How the Camel Got His Hump

Written by Catherine Coe
Illustrated by Ben Redlich

Collins

Dog and Rabbit dug the sand.

But Camel just sat.

Camel did not help.

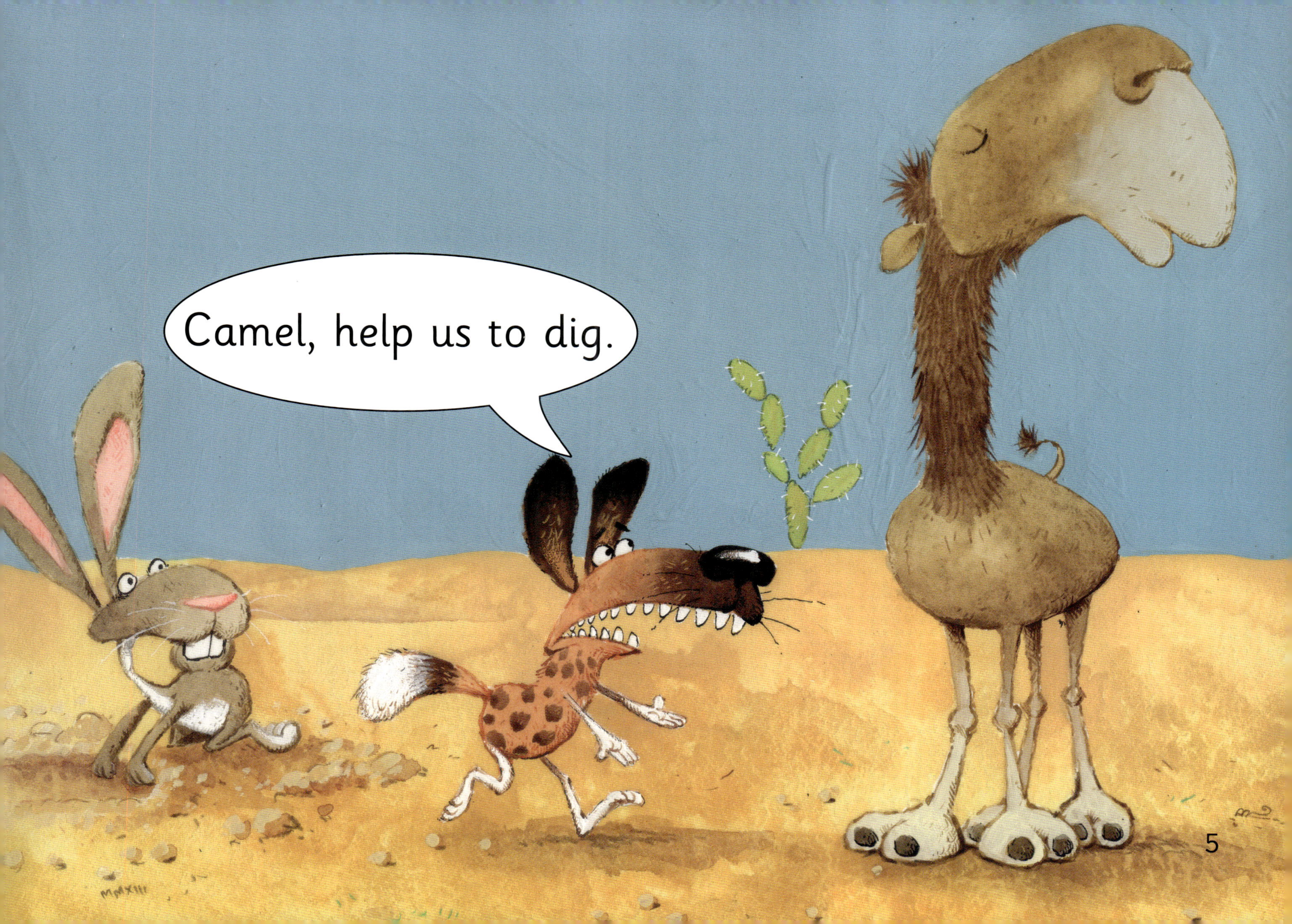
Camel, help us to dig.

Camel did not help.

Rabbit was mad. Dog was mad.

Camel had a nap.
But as he did, he got a hump!

Camel got up.

Camel was mad.

Dog, Rabbit, I will help you to dig!

Camel dug and dug the sand.

But he did not get rid of his hump!

A story map

Hump!

14

15

Ideas for reading

Written by Clare Dowdall, PhD
Lecturer and Primary Literacy Consultant

Learning objectives: *(reading objectives correspond with Red A band; all other objectives correspond with Purple band)* read simple words by sounding out and blending the phonemes all through the word from left to right; read a range of familiar and common words and simple sentences independently; give some reasons why things happen or characters change; use syntax and context to build their store of vocabulary when reading for meaning; speak with clarity and use appropriate intonation when reading aloud

Curriculum links: Geography, Citizenship

Focus phonemes: h, m, u, l, b, w, y

Fast words: he, was, you

Resources: internet, pens, paper, magnetic letters

Word count: 71

Getting started

- Ask children to tell you what they know about camels, using simple questions to guide the discussion. Explain that this book is a traditional tale about how Camel got his hump.

- Read the title and blurb together. Check that children know what a hump is and ask children to suggest how they think Camel got his hump. Sound out the word *hump* together, supporting children to count phonemes on their fingers.

- Discuss the features of traditional stories, e.g. they are set long ago; they can include a message or a lesson.

Reading and responding

- Turn to pp2–3 and look at the speech bubble on p2. Discuss how this should be read, noticing the exclamation mark.

- Ask children to read the text aloud with you. Focus on the words *Rabbit* and *Camel*. Model how to sound out each phoneme and blend the phonemes to read the words. Ask children to reread the whole sentence fluently.

- Ask children to read aloud to the end of the story, using expressive voices and rereading whole sentences fluently.